DATING

Is it worth the risk?

Reb Bradley

FAMILY MINISTRIES PUBLISHING
Sheridan, California

Reb Bradley
FAMILY MINISTRIES PUBLISHING
PO Box 266
Sheridan, California 95681
www.familyministries.com

Table of contents

INTRODUCTION

A trend has developed in the last 30 years in the area of premarital romance. Parents and young people are moving away from modern dating and returning to the tradition of parent-involved "courtship." This rejection of modern dating practices seems too radical for some parents, but others heartily embrace it. I have prepared this study for those parents who want the best for their children, and are open to the possibility that our present dating system is dangerous.

In any discussion it is always best to first define one's terms. I have prepared the following chart to clarify the difference between *dating* and *courtship*.

Defining our terms:

Courtship	Dating
1. It is engaged in for the purpose of exploring a relationship for marriage.	1. It is engaged in for the purpose of personal gratification.
2. It is a *means* to an end. It is engaged in only when ready to marry.	2. It is an *end* in itself. It is engaged in years before ready to marry, or as a substitute for marriage.
3. It requires parental involvement (except with remarriage).	3. It generally discourages parental involvement.
4. It limits the number of premarital relationships developed.	4. It provides extensive opportunities to develop multiple relationships.
5. It considers all physical contact a privilege of those who have bound themselves for life with marriage vows.	5. It promotes various levels of physical contact, from holding hands to fornication.
6. It rarely leaves couples alone or unchaperoned.	6. It provides extensive time for unmarried couples to be alone.

The key difference between courtship and dating is that *courtship* relationships are marriage-bound and *dating* relationships are not. Dating involves the pursuit of romance years before those involved are ready for marriage.

Courtship History:

Among God's people, some form of parent-involved courtship or betrothal was the primary approach to carrying on premarital romantic relationships since the beginning of human history up until the 20th Century.

Dating History:

Although pagan cultures have accepted various premarital sexual relationships, among God's people, nothing close to "dating" existed until the end of the 19th century and was not widely practiced until the mid-20th century.

A complete discussion of courtship would require an entire book or my full-day seminar on the subject, so in this booklet we will simply examine the modern tradition of dating in light of typical questions a conscientious parent might ask:

1. Does dating accomplish God's biblically established goals for my children?
    - Does it enhance their maturity?
    - Does it promote moral purity?
    - Does it best prepare them for marriage?
    - Does it keep them fit warriors for Christ?

2. Is dating based strictly on principles of premarital romance presented in the Bible?

- If it is based on "neutral" principles rooted in modern culture, are they wise and fruitful precepts?
- If rooted in culture, can practices really be neutral and acceptable, if they have a negative moral impact?

3. Is dating based on a parenting approach modeled by godly parents in the Bible?
   - What did they model for us?

In the following section we will not address each of these questions directly, but their answers will become obvious in the course of discussion.

DATING VERSUS COURTSHIP

Those who promote the modern ideas of dating over traditional courtship claim that courtship denies the benefits of dating. But *does* dating have advantages over courtship?

Does courtship deny the benefits of dating?

Those who tout what they consider to be the benefits of modern dating and criticize courtship, reject not a *modern* phenomenon, but a *time-tested* practice of godly saints, including all the parents and young people of the Bible. To broadly claim that dating serves followers of Jesus better than parent-involved courtship is to say that saints like Abraham and Sarah, Jacob and Rachel, and Joseph and Mary, were disadvantaged. To boast that dating offers superior benefits to God's people is to say that all the saints in prior centuries were lacking. Has the Church received so much good from modern dating that we can easily dismiss thousands of years of parent-involved courtship and betrothal?

Courtship has a biblical foundation

In the Old Testament the role parents played in the selection of their children's mates was presented as a positive part of the marriage process.[1] Israelite parents typically arranged marriages for their daughters,[2] or allowed interested suitors to propose. Jacob was one such young man who set his affection upon a young maiden, and spent a month getting to know her before asking her father for her hand in marriage.[3] His courtship of Rachel was not

---

[1]Gen 29:26; 34:8; 34:16-18; 41:45; Ex 2:21; 22:16; 28:32; Josh 15:16-17; Judg 1:12-13; 12:9; 21:1,7,18, 22; 1 Sam 17:25; 18:17,19,27; 25:44; 2 Ki 14:9; 1 Chr 2:35; 2 Chr 25:18; Dan 11:17

[2] Contrary to common misconceptions, a parent-involved biblical marriage was not necessarily without the consent of daughters (Gen 24:58; 1 Sam 18:20)

[3] Gen 29:14, 18

formal, but it was a courtship nonetheless.

The New Testament continues the custom of parental involvement, portraying the decision for a young woman to marry as one belonging ultimately to her father.[4] Christ himself compared his relationship with the Church to the *betrothal* aspect of courtship.[5] Can we really regard as *unwise*, those modern parents who emulate the approach presented in the Bible, or who try to follow Christ's example?

Since Adam's heavenly Father first brought him Eve, some form of parent-involved courtship or betrothal has been practiced by God's people throughout history. The Old Testament Jews, the New Testament Church, and the historical Church, all held that parents were responsible to closely oversee their children's lives, including their premarital relationships. Any kind of unchaperoned courtships did not appear until the middle 1800's. Non-marriage-bound, unchaperoned dating was not widely accepted in the Church until well into the 20th century. This is the first century in the history of the world in which

---

[4] 1 Cor 7:36-38 (KJV); Matt 22:30; Mrk 12:25; Luke 20:34-35
[5] Mt 25:1-11; Lk 5:34-35; Jn 3:29; Rev 19:7-8; 21:2,9; 22:17; 2 Cor 11:2

God's people have accepted or practiced anything like "dating."

Since dating is an invention, not of the Bible, but of a worldly society, and replaces the practices of God's people since the beginning of human history, the responsibility lies upon its advocates to prove it is good for followers of Jesus. Those who claim there are benefits to dating over courtship need to offer substantial evidence of these benefits. Can they demonstrate...

- that dating is a more effective means of keeping young people sexually pure?
- that it is morally safe and therefore a "neutral" cultural practice?
- that dating is a superior method of preparing young people for marriage than courtship has proved to be in previous centuries?
- that those who date have healthier marriages today than those who court?
- that dating enhances young people's maturity in areas of self- control, wisdom, and responsibility?
- that dating better promotes clear consciences, and keeps young people fit for maximum service to Christ?

FRUIT BORN FROM DATING
Greater sexual purity?

If this invention of the 20th century offers more benefits than historically proven and biblically modeled courtship, we should expect to see our youth today walking with greater sexual purity than in previous centuries. Sadly, the opposite is true. As parents have reduced their involvement in the courtship process over the last century, premarital sexual activity has increased proportionately.

Consider just the last 60 years. According to figures released by the U.S. Department of Health and Human Services, the percentage of sexually active teenage girls, rose from 12% in 1955 to 70% by 1988. The percentage of out-of-wedlock births to teenagers rose from 7% in 1955 to 65% in 1988. Those statistics represent a cross-section of America, but the Church isn't far behind. Josh McDowell's "Teen Sex Survey in the Evangelical Church" revealed that 43% of teens in evangelical youth groups fornicate by the time they reach their 18th birthday.[6] Dating for Christians has proven to be not just a harmless experiment in morality, but an open doorway to sexual sin.[7] This moral decline

---

[6] Why Wait Campaign, 1987.
[7] Eph 5:3

stems partly from living in a sex-saturated society, but *dating* is what gives opportunity for sexual expression.

Studies also reveal that with more single Christians having sex, 1 of every 6 abortions is performed on a professing evangelical woman.[8] Today's Christian teenagers fornicate, contract AIDS, spread venereal diseases, conceive children out of wedlock, and have abortions, because of the opportunities afforded by "wholesome," parent-approved, Christian dating. Something is drastically wrong!

Stronger marriages?

If dating better prepares young people for marriage, laying for them a stronger foundation, we should expect to see healthier, longer-lasting marriages than in previous centuries, but the troubled state of Christian marriages today speaks for itself. Marriage seminars abound, marriage books sell like hotcakes, and marriage counselors' schedules are filled, because Christian marriages are in trouble. The rate of divorce for professing Christians is almost 50%, nearly the same as secular marriages. The evidence refutes the

---

[8] Guttmacher Institute

claim that experience in modern dating lays the foundation for a good marriage. Sadly, those who stand by that claim, pass on to their children and to others, not a harmless error, but one deadly to families. The escalating death rate of Christian marriages demands that we examine the foundation laid by modern dating practices.

Perhaps, because most of us were born into a culture that predominantly builds its marriages on the foundation of dating, we have never questioned its propriety or considered finding a link between dating and the decline of marriage. But the time is at hand for pastors and parents to make such an investigation. The process that *seemed* to work for us is failing our children, and it is time to look farther back than the 1950's for premarital romantic practices that will keep our children pure and build healthier marriages. We would be wise to learn from the Scriptural pattern for premarital relationships. With rampant sexual misconduct among Christian teens, and the divorce rate for Christians on the rise, we shouldn't wait much longer.

HOW DO MODERN DATING PRACTICES CONTRIBUTE TO SEXUAL IMPURITY AND TROUBLED MARRIAGES?

Christian teens who date, clearly have more trouble with sexual impurity, and eventually experience significantly more hardships in their marriages than those who court. The causes of these problems stem from a number of factors, which are presented in the following eleven chapters.

The chart on the following page illustrates recent moral decline in the area of premarital relationships:

SEXUAL PURITY and DIVORCE among God's faithful followers through the centuries of courtship:

2000 BC Birth of Israel		1st Century AD Birth of the Early Church		19th Century	20th Century
					Dating invented by the world, adopted by the Church Sexual impurity and divorce rate skyrocketed

For centuries -- LOW divorce rate and LOW incidence of impurity.

—— 1 ——

Dating promotes lust and moderate sexual activity, opening the door for fornication.

Jesus warned his followers that simply to look upon a woman with lust was tantamount to adultery.[9] The apostle John wrote that lust of the eyes and lust of the flesh are not of God, but are of the world.[10] Peter concurred, telling us that lust is to be part of our past.[11] Paul commanded the Church to put lust to death,[12] to give their flesh no opportunity for that kind of sin,[13] and specifically told young people like Timothy to *flee youthful lusts.*[14] He also told us that within our lives, there should be nothing that even *hints* of sexual impurity, including off color jokes, or graphic discussions of sexual sin.[15] Clearly, as believers called to

---

[9] Matt. 5:27-28
[10] 1 John 2:16
[11] 1 Peter 4:3
[12] Col 3:5
[13] Rom 13:14
[14] 2 Tim 2:22
[15] Eph 5:3, 4, 12

purity, we are to avoid all lust and everything that may cause it.

The Greek language has several words for lust that each similarly mean *strong or passionate desire*. When Christians are told to eliminate lust from their lives, they are being commanded to abstain from any activity (except marriage) that guarantees the stirring of *strong sexual desires*. Considering that most steady dating relationships are characterized by some level of sexual contact,[16] it would be almost impossible to be in a relationship and not engage in lust. Any young teen who has held a date's hand or necked in the back seat of a car will confirm that it aroused *strong sexual desire*. Dating promotes the sin of lust. Rare is the teenager who can engage in sensual contact and not fall into lust. Those who do not lust are difficult to find, but if they do exist, *they should see a doctor!*

The proof that lusts are stirred in those who date are the ever-increasing multitudes of fornicating and petting young people. They may start the first date "innocently" holding hands, but their bodies respond with aroused

---

[16] Contact of a sexual nature is any that appeals to or stirs sensual desires. Includes fornication, but also holding hands, goodnight kisses, necking, etc.

lust. The fact that our dating young people fall into sexual sin should not surprise us. God designed the human body to respond powerfully to stimulation. With the Church's declining values, intense peer pressure, and plenty of alone time to provide easy opportunity, human chemistry makes sexual activity almost unavoidable. In the words of Dr. James Dobson, *"If you light the fire it's going to blaze. We're built that way hormonally."*[17]

Lust redefined

The Church today, encourages its most vulnerable members to pursue relationships that greatly foster sexual lust. Why do we do that? It would seem that we should *discourage* sin – not *promote* it. The reason for such "liberty" appears to be, because we have redefined *"lust."* In order to allow the physical relationship common to dating, we have had to call *lust* something else. The youthful lust stirred by moderate sexual activity, we now call "arousal," "low level stimulation," "hormonal excitement," "romantic intimacy," or "just getting a little turned on," but God calls it **lust** and commands us to flee it. We must call sin "sin," and teach our children to *obey* the Holy

---

[17] Focus on the Family radio broadcast, 1987

Spirit – not *tune Him out*. Feelings of conviction about lust are not "false guilt" – they are warnings to stop.

Sadly, some are so convinced that moderate sexual activity is beneficial before marriage, that they refuse to acknowledge the simple truth that *stirred sexual desires* constitute lust.

Side effects of lust

Among sins, lust is one of the most dangerous. Like fornication it is a sin against oneself,[18] but worse than fornication, it acts as the primary doorway leading to various sins. In dating, not only does it increase the likelihood of falling deeper into sexual immorality, but it severely impairs the ability to think. Those who stir their lusts will always encounter the powerful side effects. Like King Solomon, we must warn our children, *"Can a man scoop fire into his lap without his clothes being burned?"*[19] Consider some of these side effects:

1) *Lust fostered by dating – clouds one's ability to think clearly.*

One great problem produced by lust is that it blinds. By virtue of its chemical influence upon the body, it clouds one's thinking. King David

---

[18] 1 Cor 6:18
[19] Prov 6:27

20

exemplifies one blinded by the power of lust. This godly king, described as a man after God's own heart,[20] committed adultery with Bathsheba and murdered her husband because he was overcome by lust.[21] Delilah's deception of Samson presents an almost unbelievable illustration of a man who became a complete *fool* when overcome by lust. He should have seen right through her trickery,[22] but because his hormones got the best of him, he lost his eyes, his freedom, and his life.

Solomon, the wise king of Israel, provides another example of one blinded by lust. Despite his unsurpassed wisdom, he proved to be a *fool* when he forsook the living God and worshipped idols. Lust caused his foolishness. He had taken for himself 700 wives and 300 concubines, in violation of God's prohibition,[23] and he had done this despite the warnings against lust, which he had given to his own sons.[24] His lack of self-restraint led to his downfall.

---

[20] 1 Sam 13:14

[21] 2 Sam 11:2-17

[22] Judg 16:6-20

[23] Deut. 17:17

[24] Prov 6:23-35; 7:5-27; 23:26-28; 30:20

Lust: because of it, the powerful become weak and the wise become fools. As parents, we must ask ourselves – if these three godly leaders of Israel were no match for lust, should we suppose that our children will not succumb? Do we think we can send our teenagers off by themselves for romantic escapades and they won't fall victim to their natural desires? After a few generations of stirring lusts, the results implore us to stop.

2) *Lust fostered by dating – promotes self-indulgence and breaks down the self-discipline vital to purity and marital faithfulness.*

Lust is rooted in self-gratification, and therefore feeds self-centeredness. The more self-centered one becomes, the less self-discipline one has. The less one exercises self-discipline, the more one is dominated by the flesh. And the cycle continues.

The loss of a Christian's self-discipline affects all areas of life, not just the area of sexuality. Young couples who continually stir their lusts, rob one another of the inner strength needed to walk in purity of devotion to Christ. This means that they eventually enter marriage not at a place of spiritual strength, but of *weakness*. Their dating years, by fostering lust, didn't prepare them for marriage, but *hampered* their readiness. They entered marriage self-centered and lacking self-discipline. It is no wonder so many marriages start off in trouble.

Not only does the pursuit of lust spiritually cripple single Christians, but those ruled by it look to marriage as a cure for it. Most, however, are sorely disappointed. Marriage may provide a release for sexual tension, but does not automatically give its participants the self-discipline they lack. In fact, many testify that once married, they find lustful temptations grow *stronger* – not weaker.

This should not surprise us, since self-control does not come as a result of removing temptations, but blossoms as a fruit born from walking in the Spirit.[25] If a man lacked self-restraint when he was limited in sexual expression, it will not naturally come because he is free to enjoy the marriage bed. If he was undisciplined with his eyes, his body, and in his fantasies before marriage, he will find the same temptations present after marriage. Even worse, once sex becomes a normal and familiar practice, he will likely find the temptation to actively pursue sexual immorality greater than when he was single.

---

[25] Gal 5:23

Lust stirred by unmarried couples seriously *harms* them – it does not *help* them at all.

3) *Lust fostered by dating – dehumanizes, making people into objects.*

The nature of lust is self-gratification, and therefore, self-centeredness is fed by it. A self-centered person views others from the standpoint of, *"What can they do for me?"*

Men are particularly susceptible to this side effect of lust. The more a man is gratified by women, the more he views them from a selfish standpoint. To a man influenced by lust, women exist for his good. He may have the capacity for selfless compassion, but his first consideration with a woman will be *self-gratification*. She becomes in essence – an object.

Love is not self-seeking – it is considerate and respectful;[26] it is selfless and sacrificial, deferring to the other's needs first.[27] Love does not use others for personal gratification. In dating relationships, it is not *overwhelming affection* that drives a person to gratify themselves, regardless of the other's feelings or despite a possible negative outcome – it is *self-centered lust*. Sadly, many with strong romantic

---

[26] 1 Cor 13:4-5
[27] John 15:13; Phil 2:3

affection are deceived about this. They believe it is their "need" to express physical affection that drives them into the arms of the ones they date. Yet, their need is not primarily to *give* affection, but to *receive* it. The intensity with which they pursue personal gratification reflects the selfish nature of their "love." At those times, the other becomes an object to be used for gratification.

Needless to say, the self-centered view of sex fostered in lustful dating relationships causes great grief in most marriages. Individuals marry thinking the other person exists for their gratification – not just in the bedroom, but in all areas of marriage. Self-centeredness is a natural human condition and is a big enough obstacle to healthy marital love, but when it has been amplified by lust, it becomes an even greater hindrance. Should it surprise us that those who live together before marriage increase the likelihood of divorce by 50 to 100 percent?[28]

4) *Lust fostered by dating – breeds lasciviousness*

Lasciviousness is a word that describes

---

[28] William Axinn and Arland Thornton (1992), "The Relationship Between Cohabitation and Divorce: Selectivity or Casual Influence?" *Demography*, 29, p. 358.

unrestrained sexual interest.[29] It is not only lust, but it is unbridled and excessive lust. The Greek word *aselgia* literally means *preoccupation with the turning on of oneself.* Paul warned that lasciviousness is a fruit of the flesh and characteristic of those without Christ.[30]

Lust is a horrendous sin, but it is not *just* a sin – it is one that is highly dangerous, because it is *progressive.* Those who arouse their lusts by moderate sexual activity, often become *preoccupied* with continuing that gratifying activity. The more gratification they enjoy, the more consumed they become, and the more likely their sexual sin will escalate. Single Christians who continually arouse themselves, yet lack the opportunities for fulfillment afforded by marriage, can easily become lascivious. Dating promotes lascivious-ness.

5) *Lust fostered by dating – creates compulsion.*

When lasciviousness is present in someone's life, it is usually because lust has created compulsion. Like anything that gratifies, lust easily becomes habit-forming.

Young couples go out on dates, night after

---

[29] Mark 7:22
[30] Gal. 5:19-21; Eph 4:19

night, enjoying the pleasures of front seat necking. To them it seems so innocent, but eventually in their relation-ship they grow more physically intimate. They may pray together and vow that they won't give into temptation again, but when they are alone, they habitually fall. Lust rules their lives.

Men who are ruled by lust cannot drive down the street without looking lustfully at the women they see. They are preoccupied with visual gratification and consumed with satisfying their sexual curiosity. Job, as a man, understood the power of lust, so declared, *"I made a covenant with my eyes not to look lustfully at a girl."*[31] Women may also "look" at men, but often, their lust is manifested on an *emotional* level. Sensual experience offers them such a feeling of security that they begin to depend upon it for a sense of emotional wellbeing. Eventually, their dependence turns into habit. Those ruled by their habits are not ruled by Christ.[32]

In the words of the apostle Peter, *"… a man is a slave to whatever has mastered him."*[33] Those under the control of lust are not in charge of

---

[31] Job 31:1
[32] Mat 6:24
[33] 2 Pet 2:19

their lives – *lust* is. Jesus no longer "calls the shots" – *sexual passions* do. When Christian couples enter marriage, it is important that they do so ruled only by Christ. Those who begin marriage as slaves to their passions are not FREE to make wise decisions, and will lack the selfless love necessary to make marriage work. I wonder how many married couples today, are unhappy because they entered marriage mastered by their lusts, and remain self-consumed, not enjoying the freedom of Christ.

When lust rules a relationship, the individuals in it will not bear the fruit of self-control.[34] As the apostle Paul told us, *"… each of you should learn to control his own body in a way that is holy and honorable."*[35] And like Paul, we should help ourselves and our teens hold the conviction, *"I will not be mastered by anything."* [36]

6) Lust fostered by dating – defrauds.

None of us likes to be the victim of a con. In fact, most of us *abhor* being taken advantage of. Why then do we promote such defrauding for our young people in their dating? Every time a

---

[34] Gal 5:23

[35] 1 Thes 4:4

[36] 1 Cor 6:12; Rom 6:6, 16-22

couple shares moderate sexual intimacies with each other, they arouse in one another desires that cannot be righteously fulfilled. They stir lusts that can go nowhere – in essence, they defraud each other.[37] In fact, this specific characteristic of lust that intensifies the danger. No one wants to be walked down the path of arousal and then be abandoned, so farther down the path they go.

A couple defrauds one another by starting and stopping the arousal process date after date. Their bodies hate being stopped. And naturally – we were not designed to be easily switch the sexual process off and on. In marriage, aroused desire can be expressed in the marriage bed. Outside of marriage, stirred lusts have no pure place of expression. They are much like fire – safe and welcome when contained in the fireplace, but dangerously consuming when outside. Lust, like fire, can be good, but it must burn in its proper place. Outside that place of safety, it may consume every flammable thing in its path. And if it doesn't, it *nearly* will.

Another way lust causes people to defraud one another is by sending false messages of

---

[37] 1 Thes 4:3-7

commitment. For the individuals in a relationship, one may place greater meaning behind physical intimacy than the other. To them, physical involvement means sharing intimate parts of oneself that are not given to anyone else. This may mean they open their emotional receptors more than the other and misperceive the sexual affection shown them, as a symbol of the other person's love and commitment. They assume their partner is not simply using them for selfish sensual pleasure, so their hopes and expectations rise. Hearts are broken time after time, because of the false messages sent by lust.

It is the defrauding aspect of lust that leaves young women with a sense of having been used or taken advantage of. That is why so many wonder, *"Will he still respect me later?"* Lust does cause people to use each other for personal gratification. It clearly defrauds.

7) *Lust fostered by dating – creates dissatisfaction in marriage.*

For married couples, a common problem area is the marriage bed. Many complain that their physical relationship was better before they were married. Multiple surveys over the years have found similar results: couples involved sexually before marriage, often become dissatisfied once married. Why is this? The answer involves several factors, one of which is *lust*.

When we stir our lusts outside the bounds of marriage, we violate our consciences,[38] thereby gaining a sense of thrill from "getting away with something." By adding an extra measure of adrenaline to the blood stream, illicit lust increases the gratification.[39] Like the thief who shoplifts an unneeded item, simply for the "rush" of carrying out the crime, couples often find greater pleasure in physical activity when their consciences tell them it is wrong.

With the stirring of lusts enhancing premarital physical contact, many marry and eventually find themselves discontent with what could have been very satisfying. Sadly, the very lust that increased pleasure before the wedding, ultimately causes it to decrease afterwards.

8) *Lust fostered by dating – cultivates an appetite for impurity once married*

The stirring of lusts outside of marriage robs the marriage bed of some of its pleasure. As we have just discussed, many who stir their lusts

---

[38] Rom 2:15
[39] Prov 9:17; 20:17

while dating are discontent with a proper marital relationship.

Those who feed their lusts before marriage may find that they develop an appetite for impurity once married. Normal physical involvement with their spouse does not satisfy them. In search of fulfillment, they find themselves imagining in-appropriate fantasies or dredging up images of other people. Some pretend they are single again to find satisfaction. Others bring home romantic or suggestive videotapes to add missing "spice" to their own romance. This craving for a sexual supplement is not natural. It is rooted in an appetite created by illicit lust.

Because most are casualties of the dating scene, they think that all marriages need "spice" to break up bedroom boredom. Even many Christian counselors assume it is normal, so encourage it. But the self-centeredness fostered by lust in dating is the culprit. After years of marriage, some, but too few, eventually discover this truth. Their testimony is that *selfless love* is the best marital stimulant.

9) *Lust fostered by dating – leaves people with defiled consciences, weakening and rendering them spiritually ineffective.*

The Bible teaches that those who defile their

conscience destroy their faith.[40] The effect then, of multitudes of Christian young people engaging their lusts, is that each generation of young warriors for Christ are being waylaid and distracted before they ever reach the battle. Potentially frontline soldiers are being immobilized by their own hormones, and they don't even know how it happened.

Many a young couple has stumbled over this one issue. They feel confident their relationship is "pure," yet find themselves fighting back feelings of guilt over their physical involvement. They believe they are not violating any verse of Scripture, so wonder why they feel the need to "get right with God" after each date. These guilt feelings have come because God's Spirit has been faithful to convict them of sins that they are not conscious they committed. If they will listen to Him and repent, they will remain sensitive to God. But if they listen and ignore his voice, they will become callused in their conscience, and will open themselves up to far greater evil.[41] Eventually, they won't hear his conviction at all. Sadly, the latter is what most often happens.

---

[40] 1 Tim 1:19
[41] Hebrews 3:13

Young Christians have been told by the 20th century Church that the Scriptures do not forbid sharing kisses or other moderate sexual intimacies, but no one warns them that their physical relationship will immediately draw them into the sin of lust. So with their leaders' blessings and a warning to be careful, they jump into the river of lust and vainly try to swim against the current. But the Holy Spirit is there to rescue them. He tells them to turn immediately and swim back to the shore. Most ignore Him and many drown.

Certainly, it is evident that lust is nothing to play with. By every means possible we should seek to eliminate it in our children's lives. This is the first period in church history in which Christian parents have sent their children off by themselves to engage their hormones in battle. No matter how we got ourselves into this tradition, it is time to change it! Can we afford to continue sacrificing our children's purity, marriages, and souls for the sake of a modern tradition?

2

Dating develops a self-centered, feeling-oriented concept of love.

Dating is based on the idea that two people, by spending a lot of intimate time with each other, can cultivate good "chemistry" and kindle feelings of love that will last forever. This causes a problem because the emotional attraction that most people call "love" today is a "self-centered" love. Such a love says, *"I am drawn to you for how you gratify me. I like you for how you meet my needs, for how you make me feel."* Anyone in a healthy marriage will testify that *selflessness* is the key to marital health – self-centeredness and a conditional love are its downfall. Yet, the dating system, with its emphasis on physical and emotional intimacy, fosters a feeling-oriented, self-centered love.

Most who date today, engage in some level of physical intimacy in the first few dates. The resulting physical and emotional arousal can deeply affect their emotional functioning. As passions are stirred by a couple, endorphins are released into the blood stream that create an emotional "bond" between them. This bond is hormonal in nature and has little to do with true love. Sadly, many couples who create this bond eventually find themselves so gratified by it that they call it "love," and decide to marry. Once married, their expectations for gratification increase, which usually guarantees them dissatisfaction with their mates.

The excessive divorce rate among professing Christians should be no surprise today. Especially considering the self-centered love upon which most marriages are built. When couples marry because they are so gratified by each other, it means that they view a relationship from the standpoint of what they receive from it. They give to the other, but they do so with the intent of receiving something back – they expect a return on their investment. Their giving stems not from selfless love, but from self-interest. This investment-oriented love is the death of any relationship.

With couples creating hormonal bonds from the first date, it should be no surprise that they develop a self-centered, feeling-oriented concept of love. Those who challenge their hormones don't stand a chance. Following the biblical admonition to maintain the brother/sister purity[42] characteristic of courtship minimizes hormonal and emotional bonding, and offers singles a more objective, rational basis for marriage.

---

[42] 1 Tim 5:1-2

3

Dating creates a permanent romantic bond between two people who will not spend their lives together.

Dating, with its emphasis on physical and emotional intimacy, permanently knits the hearts of two people who will not be together the rest of their lives. The endorphin-based bond may fade somewhat with time, but most married people can testify to its permanence. Ex-boyfriends and girlfriends may be gone, but the emotional heart ties, along with scars and calluses, remain. Both men and women experience it. Although married many years, they may find themselves still drawn to one they "knew" in the past – the intimacy they once shared has left them with lingering feelings of closeness, familiarity, or sometimes, awkwardness.

Some discover that because of painful break-ups while single, they put up their "emotional guard" years ago, and now find themselves hampered in making the commitment necessary for a healthy marriage.

With courtship being the pattern for developing premarital relationships established from the beginning of human history, and considering the effects of going steady and breaking up, it would appear that the heart was not designed for multiple "joinings" and "tearings." Following principles of courtship minimizes premarital heart bonding and its subsequent problems.

4

Dating teaches people to break off difficult relationships, conditioning them more for divorce than marriage.

One of the "benefits" of dating is supposed to be that it allows singles to enter into multiple temporary relationships. This permits them to get to know many people and learn about life and love without binding them with any permanency. The freedom that dating offers to end troubled relationships is not a strength however, but a weakness. The teen or single adult who can break off every difficult or painful relationship subconsciously learns that they don't have to "hang in there" when the going gets tough. Not only do they not learn the selfless, unconditional love needed for a strong marriage, but instead they learn intolerance or "uncommitment." After years of breaking off challenging dating relationships, it is no wonder that so many Christians leave their own marriages when faced with difficulties. Dating does not prepare young people for marriage, but trains them for divorce. Following principles of courtship limits opportunities for excessively intimate relationships and their subsequent break-ups. This prevents any habits of "uncommitment" from ever developing.

5

Dating creates a standard of comparison by which mates are first chosen, but after marriage rejected.

Some tout as a benefit of dating that singles have the chance to be intimate with multitudes of people and thereby refine their standards for selecting a mate. This sounds reasonable until you stop to realize that the standards of comparison we use in selecting our mate don't disappear after we marry. It is not uncommon that after the newness of marriage fades and the struggles of married life start their challenge, marriage partners find themselves discontent with one another. Not uncommonly, they eventually begin to consciously or unconsciously compare their spouse to someone they "knew" in the past.

Men sometimes think thoughts like: *"She doesn't cook like so and so; She doesn't kiss as good as so and so; So and so had a better figure, and never nagged me."* Women are tempted to think thoughts like: *"He just isn't as sensitive to my needs as so and so; He just doesn't listen to me the way so and so did; Maybe I should have married so and so – he made me feel so cherished."* If we had never been intimate with others, we wouldn't have extensive standards for finding fault with our mates. We wouldn't know the difference and would find greater contentment in our marriages. It is true that we may always be tempted to compare our mates to others, but the level of intimacy created by dating increases the range and depth of those comparisons. Practicing courtship doesn't guarantee perfect marital bliss, but it does limit opportunities for developing standards of comparison.

6

Dating develops an appetite for variety and change, creating dissatisfaction within marriage.

People who use pornography, say that their appetite for stimulation is progressive – one image does not satisfy very long, so variety is needed to stay gratified. The stimulation dating offers can have a similar effect on marriages. For many singles, dating does not mean "going steady" with a few people, but going out with multitudes over a span of years. Ultimately, those who go from date to date looking for fulfillment learn to view the opposite sex as something to *gratify* them. When they do finally marry, they do so with a self-centered love, which guarantees them problems – an appetite for variety while dating doesn't disappear after marriage. For those who "played the field" while single, boredom often sets in quickly once married. Had they not dated so many, they would not have developed an appetite for variety and change. The courtship process would have protected them.

7

Dating causes late marriages, leaving more time for falling into sins associated with singleness.

Today, compared to past centuries, the average age for couples entering marriage, continues to climb.[43] Some postpone it because college must first be finished, others, because they are working to establish their careers. Some are financially able to marry, but want to "shop around" a long time to be sure they have found the best candidate for marriage. Many go steady for years because they want to be confident they are compatible with their future mate. Some singles simply find such gratification in dating that they postpone marriage indefinitely. They view marriage as something which will tie them down to one person, and which will rob them of the pleasure they find in multiple dating adventures. Dating satisfies their romantic desires, so they lack motivation to marry. The

---

[43] In 1870, the average age for marriage was 18. In 2012 it was 27.

problem with this is that the longer one dates, the greater opportunity there is to experience the failures of the dating system. Dating by itself is dangerous, but when engaged in for many years, the exposure to danger is prolonged and dramatically increases.

Christian singles today, who follow a process of courtship, are not faced with the pitfalls resulting from extended dating. A man won't even consider courting until he is financially ready to marry, so college and career preparations do not prolong premarital relationships. And within courtship there is no physical contact to stir sexual passions, so couples remain more objective and are better able to make levelheaded decisions about marriage, ending futureless relationships more quickly.

—— 8 ——

Dating destroys fellowship, leaving Christians alienated and ineffective in cooperative ministry.

Christ places a high premium on unity among his people.[44] As his followers, we therefore must do all that we can to maintain our oneness. Without it, we shame the Lord and render ourselves less effective in our outreach to the world.[45] In consideration of that, imagine the following scenario taking place at a Sunday evening youth group meeting:

Jade and Ethan have just broken up after two months of going steady. For the first time in two months, they are not sitting together. In fact, they are intentionally sitting on opposite sides of the room.

Because Jade and Ethan just broke up, Jade is joined in shunning Ethan by her two girlfriends, Ava and Chloe. Jade is so busy *not sitting* with

---

[44] John 13:35
[45] John 17:22-23

Ethan that she hardly hears a word spoken that night. Although Jade and her two friends are not speaking to Ethan, *Ashley* is.

Ashley has been waiting two months for Jade and Ethan to break up, and has wasted no time making her move. As Ashley sits by Ethan's side, Jade, Ava, and Chloe shun *her* as well. But it doesn't stop there.

Jessica is sitting at the back of the room, furious with Ashley. She has been scheming to get Ethan for weeks, and is jealous that Ashley has beaten her to the first move. In retaliation, during the announcement time, she begins spreading gossip about Ashley, which is received by eager ears, except for Ashley's friends, who are now upset at Jessica. In defense of Ashley, they now retaliate by spreading their own gossip about Jessica.

The sad part is that this is not a fictional account of an afterschool teen soap opera. Except for the names, this is a true story that has taken place many times in youth groups around the country. It is typical of the disharmony and broken relationships caused by dating. Alienation, hurt, shame, and bitterness, are almost inevitable for those who date. It is expected and accepted. But should it be?

As in marriage, dating can join a couple's hearts. And as in divorce, breaking up tears them apart. In the process, Christian fellowship is destroyed. Youth groups are full of such "divorced" couples.

As Jesus taught us, *"... a house divided against itself cannot stand."*[46] No wonder, when He interceded for his people, he prayed for their unity.[47] If we fail to maintain peace in Christian relationships, we dishonor God and render ourselves ineffective in ministry. We, therefore, should strive to be unified in all our relationships, and should do away with all that consistently causes division.[48]

Can anything be wise which causes broken relationships and hampers effective ministry? Is any activity good which has such potential to tear up the Body of Christ?[49] Absolutely not! Is it prudent then, to cling to a modern tradition that is the cause of so much trouble?

Why do we stand for this? Worse yet, why do we promote and defend it? How can the most valiant warriors in the kingdom of God be of any use in the battle, if they are at

---

[46] Luke 11:17
[47] John 17:11, 20-23
[48] Rom 12:18; 15:5; 16:17; Eph 4:3
[49] 1 Cor 1:10 -13; 3:3,17

49

constant war with or are distracted by one another? They cannot. As long as their battlefield is the conflict with other believers, they cease to fight the real enemy and take ground for the Kingdom of Light. Dating opens the door for young warriors for Christ to fall prey to Satan's schemes and be led astray from their *"sincere and pure devotion to Christ."*[50]

---

[50] 2 Cor 11:3

9

Dating lacks the protection afforded by the parental involvement of courtship.

Proponents of dating claim that traditional courtship wrongly places a parent between an adult child and God. *"After all,"* they reason, *"they are adults, with their own walks with Christ. They are the ones marrying, so they should have the chance to develop their own romantic relationships without parental intrusion. Unless they are invited in, parents should stay out of their adult children's affairs."* But as we established earlier, this line of reasoning indirectly criticizes the biblical models.

Godly parents in all past centuries played a strong, guiding role in their children's lives from birth to marriage. Would we really suggest that they were out of God's will in the area of courtship, when they maintained their parental position between their adult children and God? Do we mean to imply that *they* were over-protective and intrusive? With such bad fruit born from our "hands-off" approach to parenting, it would seem a bit shortsighted to suggest the modern Church is more *enlightened* in its freeing children from parental "interference." According to our Savior, a tree is known by its fruit,[51] and the fruit born from dating is decidedly rotten.

The tragic results of modern dating demand that we cease criticism of our godly predecessors and instead, look to them for wisdom. They, obviously, understood the parenting role better than we do. We must consider that our approach to dating may reflect a misunderstanding of biblical family structure and an error in our entire approach to *parenting*.

God created the family complete with goals, roles, and rules of operation. He held parents responsible, particularly the men, for the administration, provision, and protection of their families.[52] Biblical parents oversaw the education, training, and discipline of children,[53] and were responsible to manage them as they reached adulthood, as well.[54] God gave specific

---

[51] Mat 12:33; 7:17-19; Luke 6:43-44

[52] Eph 5:23; 1 Cor 11:8-9; Gen 18:19; Josh 24:15; 1 Tim 5:8

[53] Eph 6:4; Deut 6:6-9; 11:18-28; Prov 3:12; 13:24; 19:18; 22:6; 22:15; 23:13-14; 29:17

[54] Deut 22:20-21; 1 Tim 3:4-5; Tit 1:6; Ex 21:17

commands for children that would contribute to their maturity, prepare them to worship Him, protect them spiritually and morally, and maintain order in the home. The primary guide He gave to children was the fifth commandment. Keeping it, meant that they obeyed their parents from birth until they were released from the home, and behaved honorably toward them their entire lives.[55] It is clear from the fifth commandment, that parents do not place themselves between their children and God – God does!

Scripture gives no hint that parents were wrong to involve themselves in their adult children's lives – quite the opposite. Parents, Eli, Samuel, and David, were each held responsible by God for failing to manage their adult children.[56] God viewed strong parental involvement not as *intrusive*, but as *necessary*! Adult children must heed their parents' instructions, as evidenced by Solomon's admonitions to his adult sons throughout the book of Proverbs.[57]

---

[55] Exo 20:12; Deu 5:16; Mal 1:6; Mat 15:4; Eph 6:1-3; Col 3:20; Gen 2:24; Mat 19:5

[56] 1 Sam 3:13-14; 8:3; 1 Kings1:5-6

[57] The book of Proverbs was written by Solomon to his adult sons. Consider: *Prov 1:8 Listen, my son, to your*

When parents carefully oversaw the process of their children's pre-betrothal relationships, they did not call it "courtship." In the Bible, courtship had no name – to biblical parents it was just *parenting*. Parents simply governed their children according to common sense, from the time they were born until they were released from the home. They entrusted them with responsibilities that cultivated maturity, and protected them from temptations too great for them to handle. Courtship was a natural and logical part of protective child rearing.

Parents *must* understand the position of authority God has given them over their children. By providing strong leadership, parents do not intrude upon God's plans for children, but in fact, He uses them to direct their children's lives. This perspective for most of human history caused children to accept

---

father's instruction and do not forsake your mother's teaching; 4:1 Listen, my sons, to a father's instruction; pay attention and gain understanding; 13:1 A wise son heeds his father's instruction, but a mocker does not listen to rebuke; 23:22 Listen to your father, who gave you life, and do not despise your mother when she is old; 30:17 "The eye that mocks a father, that scorns obedience to a mother, will be pecked out by the ravens of the valley, will be eaten by the vultures.

strong parental involvement in the development of premarital romantic relationships.[58]

Unfortunately, modern parenting ideas limit parental involvement in the lives of teenage and adult children. Particularly in the area of dating, parental input is unwelcome. In fact, fathers, although charged by God with protecting their daughters' chastity,[59] are especially resented when they try to oversee or influence their daughters' relationships. This modern belief of parental "uninvolvement" has been accepted as so normal, that most parents now view the freedom to date as a "right" which they are afraid to violate.

For parents, who long ago released their teenagers to independence, re-establishing influence may be a frightening thought, but by no means need they fear *disrupting* God's plans for their teens – they *fulfill* His plans. God obviously uses parents to direct the lives of their children, or He wouldn't have commanded

---

[58] Jer 29:6; Deu 7:3; Judg 3:6; Ezra 9:12; Neh 10:30; 13:25; Prov 18:22; Gen 2:24; Mat 19:5; 22:30; Mark 10:7; 12:25; Luke 20:34-35; Eph 5:31; 1 Cor 7:36-38 [KJV]; Gen 29:26; 34:8; 34:16-18; 41:45; Ex 2:21; 22:16; 28:32; Josh 15:16-17; Judg 1:12-13; 12:9; 21:1,7,18, 22; 1 Sam 17:25; 18:17,19,27; 25:44; 2 Ki 14:9; 1 Chr 2:35; 2 Chr 25:18; Dan 11:17; Mat 22:30; Mark 12:25; Luke 20:34-35
[59] Deut 22:20-21

children to obey them. In preparation for marriage, He intends that the wisdom and discernment of concerned parents be used to guide young adults in the selection of a mate. The objective insight offered by parents in such a life-affecting decision can be invaluable, and may make the difference between a strong marriage and a broken one.

10

Dating doesn't prepare children to face "life's realities" – it *warps* life's realities!

Advocates of dating claim that courtship over-protects children from life's realities. They might even venture that courtship succeeded in all past centuries, because life's realities were not as harsh then. But they contend that it would be harmful if tried now.

Consider – which harsh realities do we have in this century that were absent in the past – rejection? abuse? overwhelming temptation? VD? unwed motherhood? abortions? broken hearts? divorce? Are our realities actually harsher than in the past? Not at all! But if in fact our realities are harsher, and our children must face these harsh realities to be properly prepared for marriage, why is it not working? We have allowed them to be surrounded with moral temptations and have permitted them to suffer the consequences of intimate relationships, but they are not better prepared for life. In fact, as the statistics reveal, sexual impurity and divorce are on the rise. There is something wrong with this hypothesis.

PARENTS – we must consider that the very "realities" for which we want our teens to be prepared are created by the dating process itself. Dating doesn't simply *expose* to life's realities – *it warps life's realities!* As should be clear from the evidence, it is dangerous to spiritual wholeness and marital health. Dating does not prepare young people for the difficulties of future life – for many, it insures that future life will be difficult.

Let us consider the questions posed earlier: Can those who support dating demonstrate . . .

- that dating is a more effective means of keeping young people sexually pure?

- that it is morally safe and therefore a "neutral" cultural practice?

- that dating is a superior method of preparing young people for marriage than courtship has proved to be in previous centuries?

- that those who date have healthier marriages today than those who court?

- that dating enhances young people's maturity in areas of self control, wisdom, and responsibility?

- that dating better promotes clear consciences,

and keeps young people fit for maximum service to Christ?

The obvious answer: NO! *Dating damages Christians.* We learn from our godly predecessors that courtship doesn't *over*-protect, but rather, it *properly* protects. Yet, many will ignore the biblical precedent, disregard the evidence, and still defend dating and criticize courtship.

It is an unusual picture, don't you think? Can you see us as 20th century Christian parents standing among a generation of self-absorbed, sexually promiscuous teens, pointing at the families with orderly, chaste children, and scolding them for being overprotective? There is something seriously wrong with this picture! It is like someone dying from lung cancer, who lies in a hospital bed touting the benefits of smoking and criticizing those who abstain.

If you wanted to keep your children sexually pure, which generation of Christians would you listen to – the one with 43% of their children sexually active, or the one with pure children? If you wanted advice on preparing your children to have strong, lasting marriages, would you seek help from a generation with a 50% divorce rate or from one in which divorce was rare?

11

Dating devalues sex and marriage.

When something holds high value, we treat it with honor and respect. We do not give it away carelessly or subject it to danger – we guard it, protect it, and preserve it. In a society plagued by divorce like ours, it is safe to say that marriage has lost the value it held in prior years. Many today regard it not as a sacred relationship to be honored and preserved for life, but one that is tossed aside when it ceases to bring satisfaction. It is yearned for with great expectation because it seems to offer such fulfillment. But once entered, marriage loses its value quickly. What has happened to make marriage so cheap and disposable? Several factors contribute to the decline of marriage, but the invention of modern dating probably contributes the most.

For most of human history, marriage was viewed as God's only relationship for the expression of romantic and sexual desires. When godly couples found themselves attracted to each other, their thoughts turned not to an open-ended dating-like relationship, but rather to *marriage* as the place for their affection. Since physical and emotional intimacies were regarded as sacred privileges of a holy union, marriage maintained high esteem in the eyes of God's people.

To biblical Jews, sacred marital privileges included all sensual touching. It was their conviction that until a couple entered a marriage covenant and swore oaths of faithfulness, they had no rights to give or receive sensual affection. Those unmarried were not to hold hands, kiss good night, share back-rubs, or spend time necking. Any affection which would be preserved for one's spouse after marriage was regarded as a *sexual privilege*, and thus was reserved for them until marriage. To the Jews, chastity meant *complete* purity, from head to toe. To godly New Testament believers, chastity meant the same. In fact, throughout Church history, up until approximately 150 years ago, the Christian community held the same conviction – all physical affection was regarded as a privilege of marriage. Those who wanted to enjoy sensuality, no matter how limited, understood that they needed to marry in order to experience it.

With the development of unchaperoned courtship in the mid-19th century, and the "recreational" dating of the 20th century, young people began to enjoy intimacies once considered to be marital privileges. Christians no longer waited for marriage to share limited sexual pleasures – they could enjoy them while single. What were formerly regarded as precious parts of marriage, in short time became cheap, common pastimes that were shared freely with many. For centuries, the Church had known what the Bible meant when it called its people to honor marriage and walk in sexual purity, but with the creation of the new *premarital sexual relationship,* purity became a "gray" area, and marriage had less to offer. This has resulted in sexual sin widely infecting the Church, and marriage being treated with contempt.

There is something terribly wrong when God explicitly calls His people to walk in sexual purity, and we respond by telling our teenagers that the Bible is not clear on what sexual purity is. Do we really think that God commanded us to be sexually pure and then left it up to us to guess about what He meant? Did He say, *"Be pure! But I'm not going to tell you what that means. It's a gray area. But you had better get it right, because I'm holding you accountable!"* Could it be that the Old Testament Jews and the New Testament Church saw clearly that which we are blind to? Is it possible that we miss the plain teaching of Scripture because we read it with the assumption that moderate sexual relationships are permissible? Are we looking to the Scriptures for guidelines to a relationship that it never considered as a possibility? Do we call "gray" that which God presented as "black and white"?

Perhaps we can learn from Paul's admonition to young Timothy: *"Do not rebuke an older man harshly, but exhort him as if he were your father. Treat younger men as brothers, 2 older women as mothers, and younger women as sisters, with absolute purity."*[60] Could it be any more clear? We must treat one another with the same degree of chastity with which we treat our own brother or sister. It is so simple. For most of its history, the Church understood this principle and enjoyed its protection. When they read, *"Be sexually pure,"*[61] they interpreted it, *"Treat one another with brother/sister purity. No good*

---

[60] 1 Tim 5:1-2
[61] Eph 5:3; 1 Th 4:4-7; 1 Cor 6:18

night kisses. No holding hands. No necking."
Today, we read, *"Be pure,"* and we interpret it
to mean, *"When you're involved with moderate
sexual affection like necking, don't get carried
away."* As long as we insist on calling sexual
purity a gray area, and allow our teens to date
and treat one another without brother-sister
purity, they will continue to fall into sexual sin
and grow in disrespect for marriage.

Dating is not a harmless cultural custom – it is
the sinister culprit that has robbed marriage of
its sanctity. It has taken privileges from
marriage and offered them to all with little
cost. It is a true saying: that which is common
and available is treasured *less* than that which
is difficult to come by. Over the last century, as
dating has increased the privileges it takes
from marriage, marriage has correspondingly
declined in value. A woman who shares her
body freely, gains the lowly reputation of a
"loose woman." Likewise, marriage has given
to dating its once sacred privileges, and in
doing so, it has lost respect and become cheap
and common.

One of the reasons that Christians in the 19th
century began unchaperoned courtship and
started sharing limited sexual privileges
outside of marriage was that maintaining

absolute purity had become an empty tradition. They had lost sight of what it was about the marriage relationship that made it so unique.

For centuries, marriage was considered to be a highly sacred relationship. In fact, marriage was so sacred, no other human relationship could offer similar rights or privileges. In order to gain its privileges, couples had to form a permanent, legal partnership, which God called the marriage covenant.[62] That covenant is similar to any legal contract that offers rights and privileges to those who willingly sign their name to a promise. Consider the following aspects of the marriage covenant, which still today should solemnize marriage:[63]

- It is a very formalized, official relationship.
- It is entered into on a contractual basis, and proscribes repercussions for violations.[64]
- The terms of the covenant or "contract" are stated in the form of vows and oaths of commitment, which are spoken before witnesses.

---

[62] Malachi 2:14; Prov 2:17

[63] Adapted from Michael Stingley, Ph.D. "*The Relevance of the Marriage Covenant in Marriage and Family Psychotherapy,*" 1985, Doctoral dissertation

[64] ie: death for adulterers: Lev 20:10; De 22:21-24

- A significant aspect of the marriage covenant is that it is consummated (made official) by a solemn oath of faithfulness, which then, and only then, allows the exercise of rights and privileges.

- Just as signing an agreement seals the terms of a contract, individuals speak marriage vows and publicly "seal" their unconditional commitment to each other.

- Wedding guests are present not just to "share in the joy" of a couple, but to act as witnesses, holding them accountable to the promises they make.

- The covenant forms an indissoluble bond between husband and wife that protects the intimate rights and privileges of their new relationship; it is as permanent as a blood relationship.

- It is a protective, formal relationship that emphasizes duty and obligation before privileges.

In the same way that signatures on a contract grant rights to the signers, speaking vows of lasting faithfulness places boundaries on a marriage relationship, and thereby grants sexual and cohabitational privileges. In the marriage covenant, a man, in essence, says to a woman, *"I will be faithful and give myself only to you,"* and the woman in return says, *"I will be faithful and keep myself for you."* And God says, *"Because you have bound yourself to a permanent union, you now have the privilege of living together and enjoying one another sexually."* Lifelong privileges are granted by God to those who speak marriage vows, because they "sign their lives away." If no vows are spoken, no privileges can be shared – if no oaths of faithfulness are sworn, no rights may be exercised. Marriage isn't just a "piece of paper" – it is a holy, God-ordained union, protected by the vows of the covenant.

It is because vows create a permanent union that Jesus declared, *"They are no longer two, but one. Therefore what God has joined together, let man not separate."*[65] When God joins a couple together in a wedding ceremony, He grants them rights to each other's bodies, and authorizes them to become one flesh.[66] By God's design, partners in a marital union ultimately "own" each other. As He told us through the apostle Paul, *"The wife's body does*

---

[65] Mat 19:6; Numbers 30:2; Deut.23:21, 23; Eccl.5:4
[66] Eph 5:31

not belong to her alone but also to her husband. In the same way, the husband's body does not belong to him alone but also to his wife."[67] The nature of the union God creates between husband and wife is difficult to fully understand or describe, but we do know that He takes *two* individuals and somehow makes them *one*. That oneness creates a new, very unique human relationship.

It is a couple's mutual ownership of each other's bodies that grants them permission for touching. According to the Bible, a wife who touches her husband isn't touching someone else's body – what used to be exclusively his is now hers, and what used to be hers is now his. When they were single they had no ownership of one another and therefore, no rights to touch. Why do we as modern Christians think we can share touching privileges without the divine union of the marriage covenant? Does it seem wise? Is it safe? Is there biblical precedent? The evidence against dating says we have not just borrowed a *harmless* custom from the world, but we have acquired one highly destructive to the Church and to marriage. In creating dating we have gutted the marriage covenant of 80% of its privileges

---

[67] 1 Cor 7:4

and in doing so, have trashed marriage of its sanctity.

Does it not seem a bit odd that, for most of history, couples had to marry in order to touch each other, yet now without cost, we grant those same touching privileges to all who date? Does it not seem presumptuous that 20th century Christians would perceive themselves as having a better way and ignore the historical understanding of the biblical marriage covenant? Compare the two systems.

Under the *biblical model* for romantic relationships, couples had almost no privileges with each other until their wedding day. In order to gain those privileges, they had to enter a marriage covenant requiring that they speak vows and oaths in front of witnesses by which they swore faithfulness and unyielding commitment to their permanent partnership. They thereby established formal, God-sanctioned boundaries to the relationship, and were united by God into a holy union.

The *modern model* for romantic relationships is much simpler. To gain its multiple rights and privileges, couples must either like each other or have some use for each other. Which model elevates marriage?

To better understand the two basic models

for romance, examine the chart on the following page. As you study it, note how the treasures of marriage have been taken by dating and spread out over years of singleness. What were once lofty privileges of a holy union are now lowly and common. The sacred has been desecrated. Those who understand reverence for the sacred are always grieved when it is dishonored. Perhaps the Israelites felt similar grief as they watched holy artifacts of the Jerusalem Temple be carried off by Babylonian conquerors.

A comparison of the BIBLICAL MODEL and the MODERN MODEL for romantic relationships.

The BIBLICAL MODEL for romantic relationships and the accompanying privileges:	The MODERN MODEL for romantic relationships and the accompanying privileges:
Age to begin:	**Age to begin:**
When ready to marry	Any age
Casual acquaintances privileges:	**Casual acquaintances privileges:**
♥ none	♥ back rubs, mistletoe kisses
Courtship privileges:	♥ slow dance full-body hugs
♥ chaperoned time together	♥ view sensual aspects of body
♥ no touching	**Dating privileges:**
Engagement privileges:	♥ moderate sexual activity, ie: holding hands, kissing, passionate hugging, face-caressing, etc.
♥ guaranteed spouse	
♥ no touching	
Marriage privileges:	♥ 1 on 1 alone-time
♥ cohabitation	♥ cultivation of emotional intimacy
♥ 1 on 1 alone-time	
♥ sexual rights, ie; back rubs, mistletoe kisses, slow dance full-body hugs, viewing of attractive aspects of body, and sexual intercourse	♥ development of social skills
	Going steady privileges:
	♥ greater sexual contact, often petting & fornication
♥ cultivation of emotional intimacy	♥ guaranteed companionship
♥ guaranteed companionship	♥ emotional security
♥ emotional security	♥ occasional cohabitation
♥ having children	♥ partial cohabitation
♥ development of social skills	**Engagement privileges:**
Requirements for gaining these privileges:	♥ increased sexual contact & cohabitation
♥ couple must enter a marriage covenant which requires that the couple speak vows and oaths in front of witnesses, swearing faithfulness and unyielding commitment to their permanent partnership, thereby establishing formal, God-sanctioned boundaries to the relationship	**Marriage privileges:**
	♥ complete cohabitation
	♥ complete sexual privilege
	♥ having children
	Requirements for gaining these privileges:
	♥ couple must like each other or have some use for each other

The treasures of marriage have been taken by dating and spread out over years of singleness.

Has marriage been robbed of its sanctity?

CONCLUSION

DATING:
CHRISTIANIZE IT OR ABANDON IT?

Dating is like a minefield laden with live bombs that destroy or wound almost everyone who enters it. If this field takes the lives of 43% of all Christian young people and wounds almost all others, why do we keep sending our children into it? Would we put our children on a plane that had a 43% chance of crashing, or give them food that had a 43% chance of being poisoned? No? Why, then, do we take risks with them morally?

Those who say, *"But we dated and we turned out okay,"* may have survived the minefield, but just because the explosions didn't kill them, does that make minefields good? Because some can be found who survive minefield explosions with minimal wounds, is that any reason to allow your children to wander in?[68]

The problem is not that teens are walking through the minefield behind our backs. They are boldly marching in with our encouragement.

---

[68] Especially since there are multiple more mines than when we were young.

And all we do, when the bombs are working their damage, is shrug our shoulders and say, *"Well, you can't protect them from real life."* Of course you can protect them! Get them out of there!

How did we ever get drawn into this morally dangerous practice?! Any objective person can see that we sacrifice our children when we engage them in it.

The serious trouble facing this present generation of young people demands radical response! We don't need more books that tell us how to improve and Christianize the worldly concept of dating. That amounts to nothing more than trying to defuse bombs in a minefield. We have been trying that for too long and the casualties are mounting up. We need to get out of the minefield! Our youth groups don't need special meetings to tell them how to recover from broken hearts. Our children need to never enter the unions that produce broken hearts! Dating leads only to the *destruction of* Christians and ministry. We need to forsake it as a failed experiment of the 20th century, and begin following the examples of our biblical forefathers.

WHY DO SOME PARENTS STRUGGLE WITH THIS TEACHING?

The negative consequences of dating are clear. Many parents, by this point, recognize the trouble facing their children, and desire to rescue them. But the thought of trying to change things at home may stir up a jumble of thoughts and questions. If that is you, perhaps you are stumbling over your fears. If you want to overcome your struggles, it may be helpful to work through the justifications that may be stumbling you. Consider the following list of reasons for practicing dating. Based on all that has been presented, the error of each should be obvious.

CONSCIOUS reasons parents struggle with this teaching

HARMLESS – They remember their own dating life and are unaware of any serious problems it created.

FUN – They don't want to deprive their kids of the fun offered by dating.

UNREALISTIC – They view courtship as an unworkable, outdated cultural practice, which cannot be implemented in a modern culture. They view it as especially impractical, in light of the excessive sexual pressure facing Christian singles and the lengthy period of time Christians must stay single before marriage.

CULTURALLY NEUTRAL – They feel Christians should look to their culture for patterns for premarital romantic relationships and not to the Bible. They consider this to be a biblical "gray area" and believe God isn't concerned about how premarital relationships are kindled. They also believe that to be an effective witness to society, Christians should be as much like the culture as possible.

AFFECTIONATE – They regard their children as very physically affectionate, so wouldn't want them to be stifled in giving or receiving affection. Courtship would prevent children from having an avenue of expression for romantic and physical desires.

TOO DIFFICULT – If they were young, they couldn't imagine themselves exercising the self-control necessary for courtship, so they don't want to require of their teen something that they themselves wouldn't want to do.

MARRIAGE PREPARATION – They believe multiple dating relationships will best prepare their kids for marriage, and are ignorant of evidence to the contrary.

FEAR CONFLICT – Their teens are already actively dating, so they fear that any attempt to implement courtship would cause major conflict, and possibly cause their child to alienate himself or even run away from home.

PEER PRESSURE – They don't want their kids to experience rejection from their peers, so they refuse to consider courtship or any Christian practice that might bring them persecution.

DEFER TO LEADERS – Some, after learning the dangers of dating, may offer no justifications for embracing it, but still embrace it anyway. The only reason they cite is that many Christian leaders accept the practice. It doesn't occur to them that possibly those leaders have never studied the dangers of dating. (That is like seeing a leaky boat starting to sink, but remaining aboard, because a respected Bible teacher is on board for a cruise. Such blind trust may mean the drowning of one's children!)

UNCONSCIOUS reasons parents struggle with this teaching

DEFENSIVENESS – Accepting courtship as best for our children requires that we acknowledge we have erred in the past. We as parents are sometimes defensive about our parenting, so rather than consider we have done something wrong, we defend the dangerous and immediately attack the helpful. Those who are unwilling to consider they have been wrong about dating may defend it despite the evidence against it. They may even attack the wisdom of courtship, and conveniently label it "legalism."

BARGAIN LOVERS – Why do we resist what will bring so much good?! Is it that we want our children to have fun without consequences? Do we want for them rights without responsibilities? Most teenagers love dating and would abhor the thought of its abandonment. And why not – it offers most of the privileges of marriage, but without the commitment. What a bargain! Pleasure can be had with minimal immediate cost. We endorse dating for our children because we love a bargain and don't want our children to have to return to the days of paying "full price." Our modern system of dating is appealing to *our* flesh, as well as our children's!

FEAR OF CHANGE – Courtship seems too new and too weird. They have always believed in dating as an acceptable modern tradition and find it difficult to do something so "radical." Some people don't like any kind of change. They unthinkingly accept society's traditions and simply try to Christianize them. In fear, they close their eyes to the indisputable dangers of dating, put their fingers in their ears and say something like, *"Well, I still think dating is fine. It's all cultural!"*

CRAVE APPROVAL – Thoughts of accepting courtship cannot even be entertained by some parents. They crave their children's approval and fear they will lose it if they try to interfere with their dating life.

FEAR OF CONTROL – The most pervasive reason that parents struggle with courtship centers around their fear of exercising control. They have not practiced exerting strong parental leadership, so are not ready to assert the firm control necessary to implement courtship. Having already shared their parental authority with their teenagers, they are afraid to take it back. To change this area of parenting their teens will require modification of their *whole* approach to parenting. They feel ill equipped to do so, and dread the outcome.

SELF-CENTERED – Few parents are willing to consider that self-centeredness may stand in the way of their parenting. But the truth is that we as parents may value our own comfort, or the fulfillment of our personal ambitions, more than we do our children's well being. We may endure great tension with our teens and feel like we daily sacrifice our peace of mind, but some of us have never been willing to give the time and energy required of sacrificial parenting.

PARENTS, when our children were young, did we choose a better income over time with them? Did we frequently overlook misbehavior because we didn't feel like giving the time or energy required of proper discipline? Did we withhold needed chastisement because we didn't want to hear our children cry, or because we wanted to appease our guilt feelings for being away from them during the day? Did we do our children's homework for them because it was easier than trying to teach them to do it themselves, or were we too busy with our own life to help with homework at all? Do we now allow our children to watch questionable TV shows, listen to godless music, and spend time with the wrong friends, because it is more peaceful than arguing or enduring their complaints? PARENTS, we must consider, do we resist courtship because it calls us to a level of involvement with our children that we have never been willing to make?

PARENTS – which of these are good enough reasons to risk your teens' moral purity and the health of their future marriages?

Is it possible today?

Can you imagine what it would be like if the Church successfully re-elevated their view of the marriage covenant and returned to some form of parent-involved courtship? Young people would walk in greater sexual purity. They would not be stirring their lusts and suffering its side effects. There would be less fornication, fewer incidences of VD or AIDS, reduced numbers of out-of-wedlock children, and the abortion rate would drop. Young people would make wiser choices in marriage partners, would likely be happier in marriage, and more faithful to their spouses. Pastors would spend less time in marriage counseling. Fewer marriages would end in divorce. Single Christians would walk with clear consciences and could minister more effectively with their peers. The Church would not be a utopia, but we would be able to move away from the some of the spiritual conflicts and moral problems that distract us from the real battle for the Kingdom of God.

Practicing principles of courtship is possible in today's culture. Tens of thousands nationwide are now doing it, and the numbers of those starting the path increase daily. By no means is courtship unworkable in our society. Many who were raised with its principles are now married and are reaping the blessings. To institute courtship with teenage children will require many parents to completely change the way they parent, but those who equip themselves will succeed.

REVIEW

How do modern dating practices contribute to sexual impurity, troubled marriages, and spiritual impotence?

1. Dating promotes lust and moderate sexual activity, opening the door for fornication.

2. Dating develops a self-centered, feeling-oriented concept of love.

3. Dating creates a permanent romantic bond between two people who will not spend their lives together.

4. Dating teaches people to break off difficult relationships, conditioning them more for divorce than marriage.

5. Dating creates a standard of comparison by which mates are first chosen, but after marriage rejected.

6. Dating develops an appetite for variety and change, creating dissatisfaction within marriage.

7. Dating causes late marriages, leaving more time for falling into sins associated with singleness.

8. Dating destroys fellowship, leaving Christians alienated and ineffective in cooperative ministry.

9. Dating lacks the protection and guidance afforded by parental involvement of courtship.

10. Dating doesn't prepare children to face "life's realities" – it *warps* life's realities!

11. Dating devalues sex and marriage.

FOR FURTHER HELP
ON THE SUBJECT OF COURTSHIP:

This book is not intended to be a complete study on Christian courtship. It is simply a wake-up call to the Church to examine recreational dating as an acceptable practice for our young people. We must rescue this next generation of young people before it is too late. For parents who desire a thorough presentation on the subject of courtship, including a practical plan for implementing courtship principles, I recommend the seminar, **Preparing Your Children for Courtship and Marriage: From toddlers to teens**.

Preparing Your Children For COURTSHIP and MARRIAGE: *From Toddlers to Teens*

How do parents accidentally lead their children into sexual impurity? This series exposes for parents which practices of modern dating contribute to sexual promiscuity and build a foundation for unstable marriages. It offers a plan for shaping children's sexual and romantic *values* from the time they are young. Especially valuable for parents of young children.

8-disc CD $46 ----- **7-disc DVD set** $90
(Free syllabus available as download)

(800) 545-1729 ❖ www.familyministries.com

Materials by Reb Bradley

Preparing Your Children for Courtship and Marriage: *From toddlers to teens.* 8-CD/DVD *set*

Parenting Teens With the Wisdom of Solomon: What the Bible Says About Raising Teenagers – *CD/DVD set*

Influencing Children's Hearts – 4-CD set

Child Training Tips: *What I wish I knew when my children were young – softbound book*

Biblical Insights into Child Training Establishing control in the home and raising godly children – 8 *CD/DVD set*

Solving the Crisis in Homeschooling: Exposing seven major blind spots of conscientious parents that increase prodigal tendencies in children; book

The Delightful Family – How to create strong family bonds, raise joyful children, and minimize sibling rivalry – 3 *CD set*

Powerful Christian Living: *Following Jesus into Wholeness.* Amazing series revealing Jesus' path to Christian maturity – *12 CD set*

Motives of the Heart: A biblical study in pride and humility *(very revealing) – 3-CD or 6-DVD sets*

Reconciling With Your Wife: Critical help for the husband who finds himself abandoned by his wife – *booklet*

For these materials and many others, contact your source for this book, or request a complete catalog from Family Ministries at 800-545-1729.
www.familyministries.com

Made in the USA
Charleston, SC
26 April 2013